YOUNG ELI READERS

Jane Cadwallader

Harry and the Crown

Illustrated by Gustavo Mazali

Harry was a policeman. One day, the Chief wanted to see him and a policewoman called Emma. All the detectives were a little afraid of the Chief. He was clever but he didn't smile very often! The Chief pointed to some photographs and said, 'I want you to catch the Rucksack Gang. They're going to rob the Castle Museum tonight.'

'Great!' said Emma happily.

'Hmmm,' said Harry.

The Chief showed Emma and Harry two rings and a computer. On the computer screen you could see where the rings were. The Chief said, 'Wear these rings. We can see where you are!'
Emma said, 'Good idea Chief!'
Harry looked at the rings. He wanted to be at home eating ice-cream in front of the television! His legs felt weak. He wasn't feeling very brave!

Harry and Emma put on the rings and went to the Castle with Betty and Robert. Betty and Robert were wearing their police uniforms. They waited in the car with the computer while Emma and Harry went into the Castle. 'See you later!' said Betty. 'Good luck! We'll watch you on the computer!' said Robert.
'Thank you!' said Emma.
'Hmmm!' said Harry.

‘Come on Harry! I have an idea!’ said Emma. Harry was not happy! He didn’t like working with Emma. She was always running around! Harry liked to live quietly. Emma gave Harry some armour to wear. ‘With the armour on we can see the robbers but they can’t see us! It will be easy to catch them!’ said Emma.

‘Hmmm!’ said Harry.

Emma helped Harry to get dressed. Harry's ring got caught on a metal vest. 'Ouch! Stop pulling!' said Harry.
'Oh! O.K. Sorry!' said Emma.

Harry took the ring off and put it onto a crown. He was NOT happy! He said, 'I don't think this is a very good idea! This armour is very heavy!' But Emma just said, 'Please be quiet Harry! We're going to catch the robbers and the Chief is going to be very happy with us!'

Emma got dressed in her armour too. They tried to move quietly but the walls and floors were made of wood and when they moved there was a loud *CLUNK CLUNK CLUNK*.

Harry looked around.
He thought, 'What were the Kings and Queens who wore these crowns and jewellery like?'
Suddenly he had a horrible idea. 'I hope there aren't any ghosts here!'
'I'll wait in the hall,' said Emma and *CLUNK CLUNK CLUNK*, off she went.

It was very quiet. Harry was bored. Bored AND hungry. He went *CLUNK CLUNK CLUNK* over to the door. He looked into the hall. Emma was sleeping. 'Ah ha!' thought Harry, 'Emma is sleeping!'

Harry wanted a snack. Then he remembered he had a piece of pizza and a plastic bottle of lemonade in his bag. He took them out and started to eat and drink … or rather, he TRIED to eat and drink! 'This is difficult!' thought Harry.

And then he invented a dance.

▶ 3 *Put your elbows up*
Stamp your feet on the ground
Make circles with your shoulders
And turn around
Do the Armour Jive
And count to five
1 2 3 4 5 HEY!

Bend your knees
Stamp your feet on the ground
Pat your stomach
And turn around
Do the Armour Jive
And count to five
1 2 3 4 5 HEY!

4 Suddenly Harry heard a noise. Emma came into the room with a bag. She began to collect the gold and silver and jewels. Harry laughed. 'That's a good idea Emma. Ha Ha! If there aren't any jewels, the robbers can't STEAL any jewels! Well done!'

Emma put the things made of gold and silver and jewels into the bag. Harry pointed to a crown. He said, 'Don't forget that crown Emma! It's got lots of jewels!'

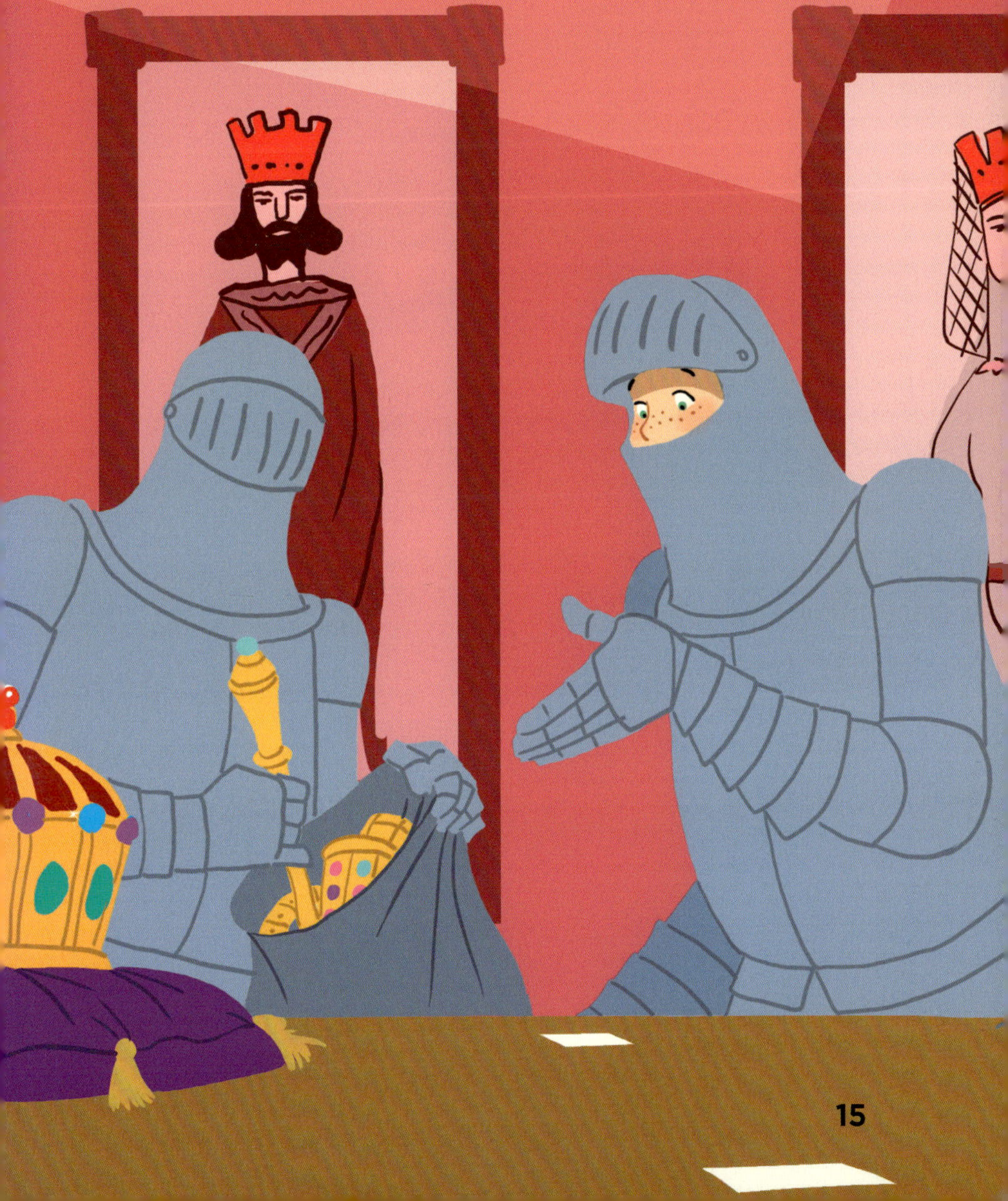

Emma left the room and Harry went on waiting. He was bored and he felt hungry again! Harry thought, 'I think I'll just close my eyes for a minute.'

Suddenly Emma was talking to him. 'Harry! Harry! The robbers aren't coming. Let's go home!' Harry was very happy! 'I agree!' he said. 'Don't forget to put the jewels back before we go Emma.'

Emma was horrified! She didn't have any jewels! Her mouth opened and she looked at Harry. Finally she said, 'What jewels? What are you talking about?'

Harry looked at her in surprise. 'The jewels you put in your bag.' Suddenly a terrible thought came into Harry's mind … 'OH NO!'

Harry felt terrible! What was he going to do? Suddenly he had an idea. 'Hey! Emma!' said Harry. 'I've got an idea! The ring! The ring I put on the crown! Quick!'

Harry and Emma ran outside. They ran to the car. Betty and Robert were surprised. At first they thought two ghosts were coming out of the Castle but then they saw it was Harry and Emma. Harry said, ‘Quick! Betty! Turn on the computer!’

Emma added, ‘The robbers have got the jewels! We must follow the signal!’

The detectives looked for the signal. There were two signals. 'Oh no!' said Harry. 'There are two signals! How do we know which is the right one?' Emma looked at him. 'Because the other one is mine Harry!'

Robert pointed to the two signals. 'This is Emma's signal and this is Harry's.' The signal was coming from North Street. If the signal was there, the ring was there and if the ring was there the crown was there, and if the crown was there THE ROBBERS WERE THERE!

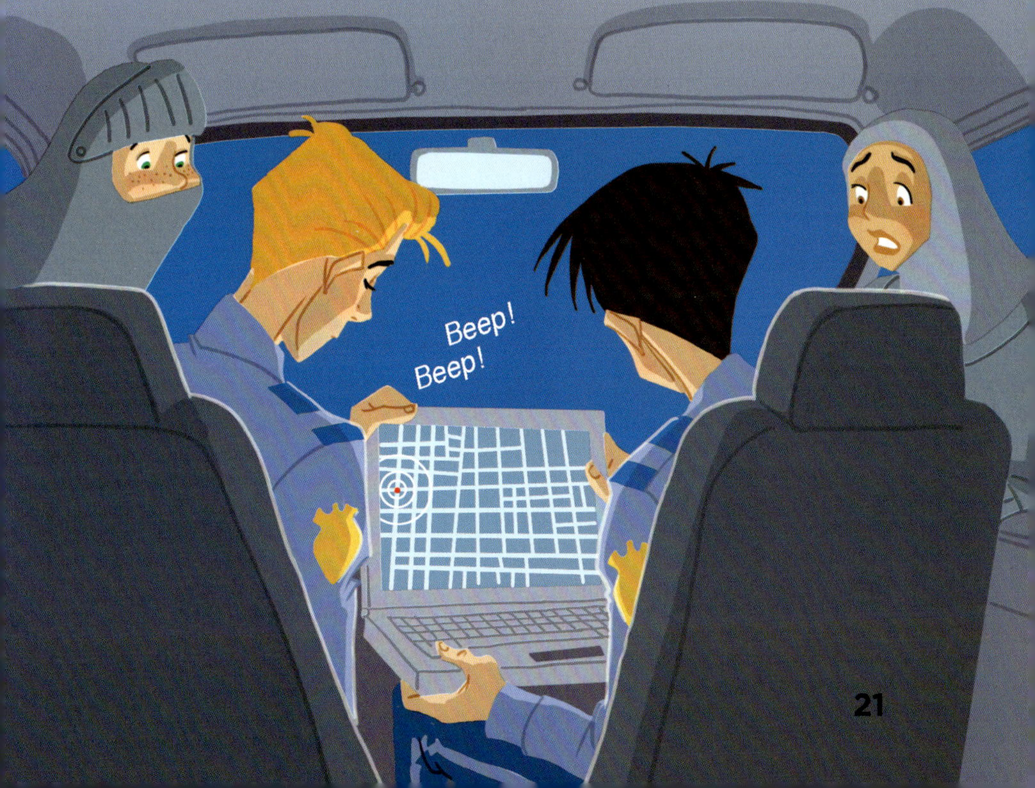

Robert said, 'O.K. Quick. We must go straight on and then go right at the post office. Then straight on and left at the station. Then straight on and right at the factory.

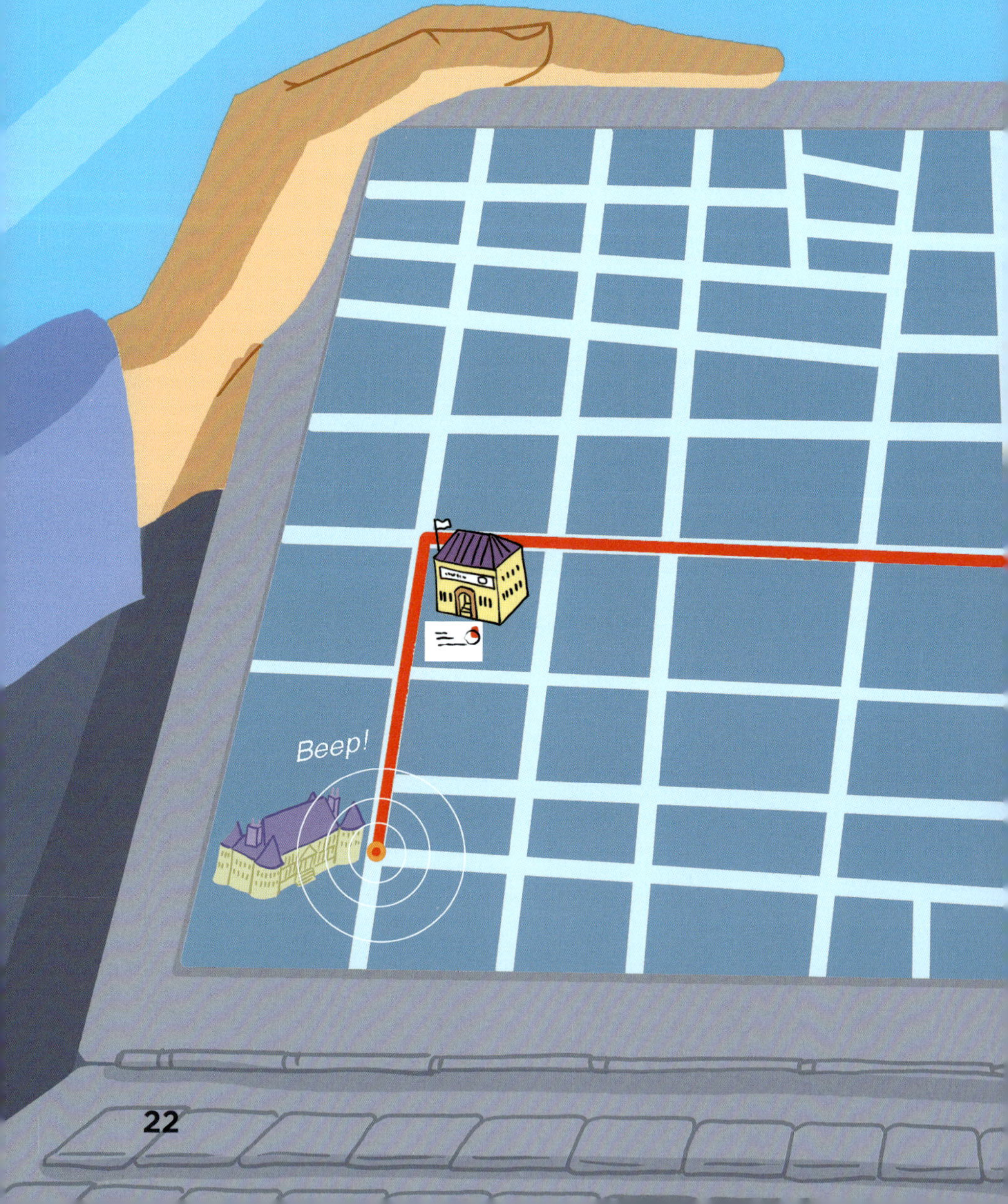

Then over the bridge. The first street on the left is North Street. The signal is coming from the fourth house on the left.'

Betty said, 'Let's go! Get in you two!'

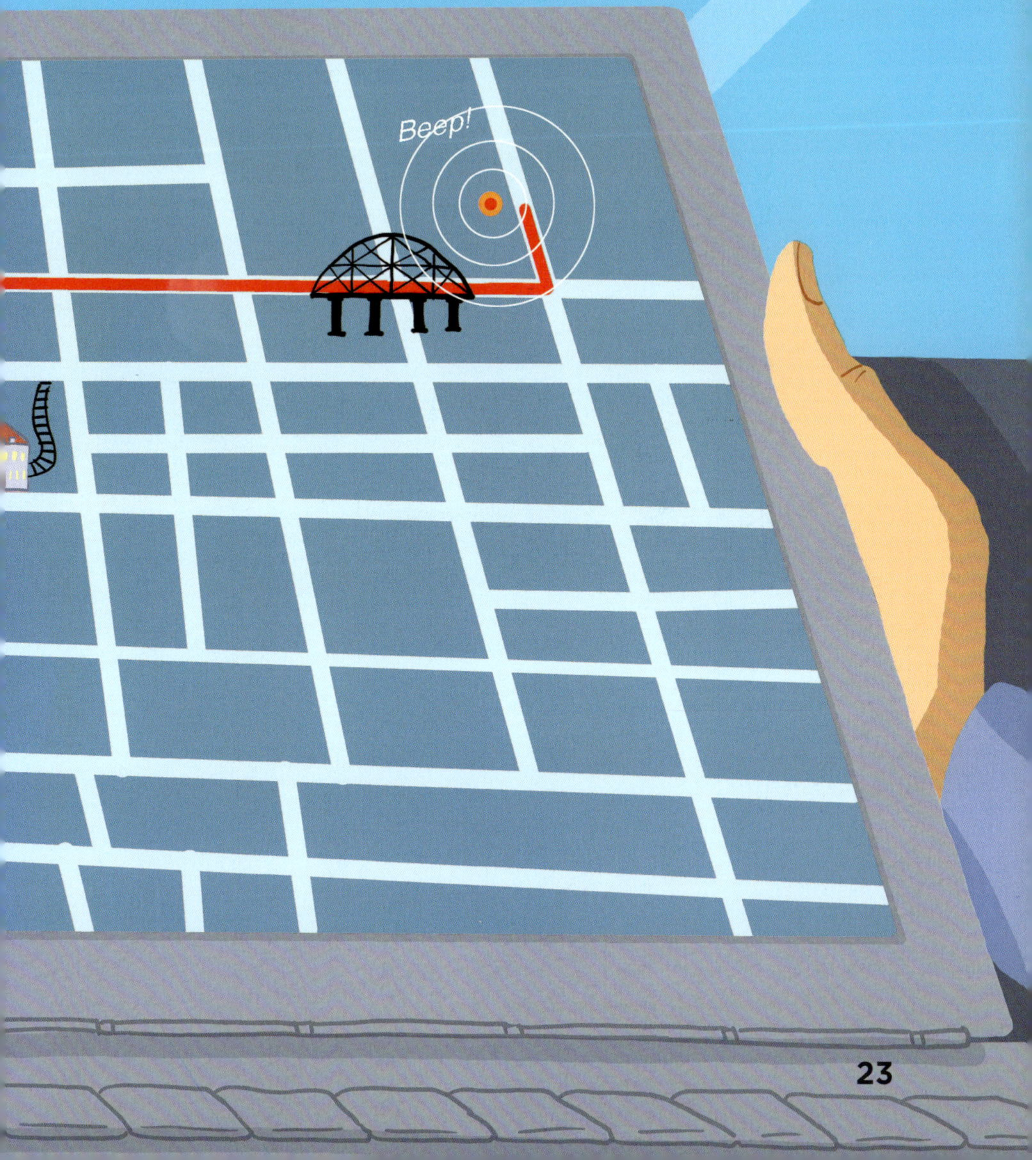

When the detectives arrived at the house of the robbers they were talking about the Castle Museum. The man said, 'When I went into the room with the Crown Jewels there was a ghost in armour. He spoke to me!' The woman replied, 'Don't be silly! Ghosts don't exist!'

The detectives jumped into the room. 'Look!' said the man, 'There it is! There's the ghost!' 'Oh!' he said, seeing Emma, 'There are two of them!'
Emma looked at him. 'We aren't ghosts, we're detectives! Come with us please!'
Harry was busy looking for the jewels. 'Have they got the Crown Jewels? YES! Thank goodness!'

That afternoon Harry and Emma went to see the Chief.

5 Karaoke music

Activity Pages

1 Write the words. Use the words to fill the gaps.

Harry rucksack Harry Chief jewels
~~ring~~ armour crown ring Harry

1 Harry put the ___ring___ on the ________ .

2 Harry and Emma wore the ________ .

3 ________ sang a song.

4 The robber took the ________ and put them in his ________ .

5 ________ and his friends followed the signals from the ________ to find the robbers.

6 The ________ was very happy with ________ .

2 Cross out the wrong word. Match the lines in the song.

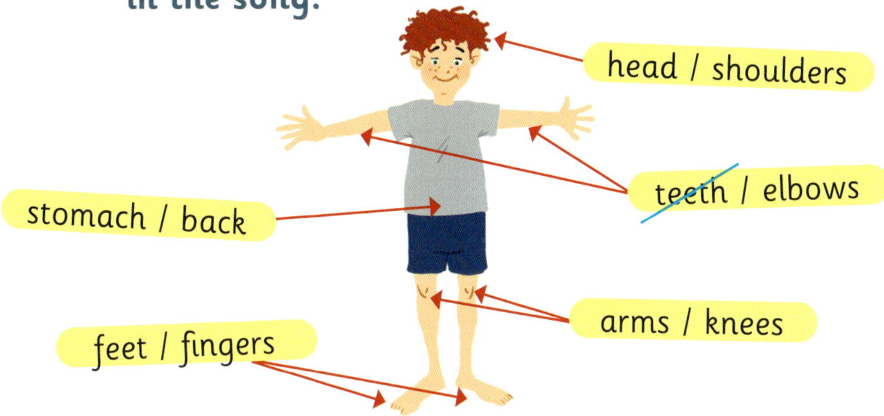

Put your	shoulders
Stamp your	jive
Make circles with your	elbows up
And turn	to five
Do the armour	Hey!
And count	around
1 2 3 4 5	feet on the ground
Bend your	stomach
Stamp your	around
Pat your	knees
And turn	to five
Do the armour	feet on the ground
And count	Hey!
1 2 3 4 5	jive

3 Find the materials the objects are made from. Write.

A	T	G	M	J	M	P	H	T
W	O	O	D	S	E	R	S	W
L	P	L	A	S	T	I	C	T
V	C	D	B	X	A	Z	F	I
E	G	U	S	I	L	V	E	R

1 This ring is made of gold .

2 This ______ ______ ______ ______ ______ .

3 This ______ ______ ______ ______ ______ .

4 This ______ ______ ______ ______ ______ .

5 This ______ ______ ______ ______ ______ .

4 Match the words. Write them in the correct column.

Lem seum tle Piz Cas tory
Ice-c ~~Sn~~ za onade Fac ream
Mu dge ~~ack~~ Bri

Food	Places
Snack	______
______	______
______	______
______	______

5 Use the clues to write the sentences.

	1	2	3	4
A		woman	turn left	
B		Harry		tonight
C		castle	police station	

(2B - 1C - 1B)

1 Harry ate pizza and drank lemonade.

(1A - 3A - 3C)

2 ______________________

(2A - 4A - 4C)

3 ______________________

(2C - 3B - 4B)

4 ______________________

6 **Draw and describe other things which Harry and his friends found in the robber's house.**

In the robbers house Harry found the jewels and the crown from the Castle Museum. He also found:

7 **Did you like the story? Draw your face and choose a sentence to write.**

I liked it.

I loved it.

I didn't like it at all.

I didn't like it much.

I quite liked it.